CW00954303

THE INFINITE MOMENT

THE INFINITE
MOMENT

Poems from Ancient Greek
Translated by Sam Hamill

A NEW DIRECTIONS BOOK

ACKNOWLEDGMENTS
Thanks to the editors of *Tri-Quarterly* for publishing the poems of
Sappho; to the editors of *Willow Springs* for publishing the poems of
Alcaeus; and to the editors of *Colorado North Review* for publishing
the *Lyra Graeca* poems.

Manufactured in the United States of America
New Directions Books are published on acid-free paper.
First published as New Directions Paperbook 738 in 1992
Published simultaneously in Canada by
Penguin Books Canada Limited

Library of Congress Cataloging in Publication Data

The Infinite moment : poems from ancient Greek / translated by
Sam Hamill
p.   cm.
ISBN 0-8112-1199-1 (pbk. : alk. paper)
1. Greek poetry – Translations into English.   I. Hamill, Sam.
PA3622.H36 1992
881'.0108 – dc20   91-44138

New Directions Books are published for James Laughlin
by New Directions Publishing Corporation,
80 Eighth Avenue, New York 10011

To Tree Swenson and Eron Hamill

and to Freeda Hamill who introduced me to the classics

CONTENTS

Sometime around 600 B.C.E., a young woman on the island of Lesbos wrote a love poem in which she confessed:

> Eros seizes and shakes my very soul
> like the wind on the mountain
> shaking ancient oaks.

Perhaps there are other shards from this poem among the many fragments that have survived the ravages of 2500 years. Or perhaps not. Nonetheless, whether we take these "lines" as only a fragment or whether we choose to read them as an entire poem (as I would present them), the poet has, in a metaphor, captured a universal human experience in an infinite moment.

The poet, Sappho, was born on Lesbos about 630 B.C.E. and raised in a wealthy family that included at least three brothers. We know from the Parian Chronicle that she was exiled to Syracuse for political reasons sometime between 604 and 596 B.C.E., that she bore a daughter, Kleis, and that she returned to Lesbos after a general amnesty was granted all political prisoners and

exiles in 581. And we know that what has made it pos-
sible for her fragments to inspire readers and poets
through all these centuries is that her words touch
something fundamental in the experience of each of
us – call it love or longing or desire.

Unlike her younger contemporary, Alcaeus, her
poems offer almost no overt political commentary.
Besides her many rhythmic inventions and adapta-
tions, her greatest contribution to poetry lies in her
ability to speak in a distinctly personal voice whether
offering a prayer to the Goddess of Love, Aphrodite,
or lamenting the absence of her (real or imaginary)
lover. This is a voice that transcends time and place:

> The Pleiades disappear,
> the pale moon goes down.
>
> After midnight, time blurs:
> sleepless, I lie alone.

This poem could be a translation from the Sanskrit
or Chinese or Japanese or even from some prehistori-
cal glyph. But it is Sappho, and while the poem works
as a whole and complete unit, it was brought from
some larger context that has been lost forever. And
there is poetry in that, too.

If we know almost nothing about the day to day
details of the life of Sappho, we know even less about
many of the other early Greek poets. What we know

of the life of Alcaeus, for example, comes mostly from his political nemesis, the tyrant Pittakos, who was identified by Aristotle as an "elected tyrant," that is, one to whom autocratic power was openly granted by the *polis* rather than having been seized through violence. Even the dates of Alcaeus are uncertain; evidence suggests that he was born sometime around 620 B.C.E. There is no evidence to suggest that he lived beyond 580 B.C.E. We can be certain only that he was roughly contemporary with and slightly younger than Sappho.

He provides a distinct contrast to Sappho's extremely personal verse. "I despise love," he says, and we may assume that his comment is not merely ironic. He is a political poet longing "for the call to council" that will return to the son his father's stolen lands. And like Sappho, he was an exile. Nonetheless, there is a magnificent *joie de vivre* in these poems, a spirit of emotional honesty and a responsiveness to the immediate world that is universal. Anakreon's is a *carpe diem* ("Seize the day!") of an unusual kind. He thumbs his nose or salutes with a middle finger. He is "concerned only with the moment," with covering his head "with a garland of roses." His contempt for conventional power is zen-like in its insistence upon making the most of the moment:

> Who cares about the filthy rich
> excesses of the Boss of Sardis?

>   He's nothing to me. I won't
>   be bothered with tyrants.

And he closes his poem with a rich invective:

>   Soon enough a day will come
>   bringing consumption or diseases.

Throughout these poems and fragments, we glimpse the unchanging nature of fundamental human tragedy and comedy. When Parmenion says,

>   For a little gold, Zeus bought Danae.
>   I, likewise, would buy you.
>   But I won't pay more than Zeus.

even those for whom Greek mythology is utterly unknown territory can appreciate the poem's humor and pathos. And when some anonymous poet says to his love,

>   The very God of Love
>   will stroke your hair
>   when it is gray,

we can still glimpse today the profound difference between mature adult love and young lovers' barely containable passion.

Rufinus may have been the first poet to introduce

the subject of domestic violence to poetry when he wrote:

> How can any man throw out
> a woman in her negligee
> just because
> he finds her with a lover?

He points to a double standard, and soothes the distressed woman ("Don't spoil your face with tears,/ my child, don't cry . . . ") and offers to help find her a more suitable paramour, "a man with gentle eyes/ who would never beat a child." Rufinus treats a terrifying subject, but makes it more palatable by trying to retain an almost desperate sense of humor while simultaneously offering compassion.

Callicteros offers a couplet: "There's wheat at home where you didn't leave it?/ Your wife has a big horn of plenty." Secret love and infidelity are frequent themes in ancient Greek lyrics, but if the occasions of love are the paradigm of Greek poetry, they are often spiced with salty humor:

> I don't refuse that kiss
> because you lick the sugar cane,
> but because the sugar cane is practice.
> — AMMIANUS

Elsewhere, especially in the epigrams, there are poems full of good, common-sense advice, and loaded with a healthy invective as well. But beauty and virtue remain the central ideas of the age. Marcus Argentarius tells us:

> Looking and lusting is not love.
> He who trusts his eyes too much is blind.
>
> But he who sees in a homely face
> the beauty and the light beneath—
>
> he knows the furnace of love's fire.
> Beauty touches those who know its form.

When Sappho sings of loving "love's delicacy," she directs our attention to love as light with the brilliance of a sun, and, in her own ineluctably Greek way, to "the virtue/ of its beauty." For the classical poets, beauty and virtue are possibilities embodied by each of us and capable of being expressed in poems that are often unself-consciously direct, simple, even spare, but highly sophisticated. For the early Greeks, the idea of virtue did not carry the kind of religious overtones the word assumes in contemporary American English. Aristotle identified the source of *virtu* as "social conscience" (*politike arete*) that has as much place at the hearthfire as in the political arena. In a didactic poem from the *Lyra Graeca*, Bacchylides offers this advice:

> Learn from others
> their multitude
> of skills.
>
> There are no words,
> invented or willed,
> that were unused
> before.

Nor are there any new emotions. The lyric poem was meant to be presented in a social context with musical accompaniment, usually a lyre or a "reed flute" or with some assortment of instruments. The lyric poet, then as now, struggled to articulate the experience of insight attained during the infinity of the moment. For more than two millennia, we have returned to ancient Greek poetry, both in the original and through translation, to taste again those rich waters that nourished roots from which so many cultures have blossomed. And within the poems and fragments we have discovered something essential about ourselves.

SAPPHO

He is almost a god, a man beside you,
enthralled by your talk, by your laughter.
Watching makes my heart beat fast
because, seeing little, I imagine much.
You put a fire in my cheeks.
Speech won't come. My ears ring.
Blind to all others, I sweat and I stammer.
I am a trembling thing, like grass,
an inch from dying.

So poor I've nothing to lose, I must gamble . . .

✛   ✛   ✛

I longed to
embrace you
so long ago
when you
were still a
graceless girl.

If you had lusted after something noble or decent,
had you not filled your talk with the vile—

had you told the truth, shame would not
force you to turn away your eyes.

✛   ✛   ✛

All the stars turn away their faces
when the pale moon grows full,
who, in her splendor,
turns the wide, shining world
into silver.

Eros seizes and shakes my very soul
like the wind on the mountain
shaking ancient oaks.

✛   ✛   ✛

When rage invades your burning breast,
restrain your tongue: it is a beast.

✛   ✛   ✛

As the full moon slowly rose,
women rose before it
as though it were an altar.

At last, on delicate feet,
the women of Krete

dance 'round the altar,
tromping down soft summer grass.

✛   ✛   ✛

Silent on the subject of vengeance,
I cling to innocence.

Must be some girl from the villages
has hypnotized your heart:

some tart who's yet to learn
how and when to drop her dress!

✛   ✛   ✛

Someday you will be dead.
Even our memory of you will die.

You think you've earned a wreath
of laurels to crown your pretty head?

Unknown even as you wander
the infinities of Hell, you belong

among the shadows of the dead.

High on the upper, outermost bough,
the sweet apple blushes.

Below, the party-goers saw, thirsted,
but could not touch it.

✛   ✛   ✛

Muse of the Golden Throne,
raise your voice again to sing
that song learned from the Sage of Teos,

that song of ample land and fair women
his sweet singing
made palpable, a gift for us.

I love
love's delicacy.

Love offers me
this brilliant sun,

the virtue
of its beauty.

✛   ✛   ✛

Here lies the dust of Timas,
borne to Persephone's darkness
before her wedding day.

When friends joined to mourn her,
they dressed alike, honed steel
glinting in their tresses.

The Pleiades disappear,
the pale moon goes down.

After midnight, time blurs:
sleepless, I lie alone.

ALCAEUS

. . . Her heart so stricken, Helen
clutched her breast and wept for Paris
as he, in turn, deceived his host;
and she stole away on his boat,
abandoning her child and her husband's bed . . .

And now how many brothers of Paris
lie planted in black earth
across the plains of Troy?
All for that woman, chariots ground to dust,
noble, olive-skinned men all slaughtered
on her behalf.

I long for the call to council
that I will never hear.

Driven from the land that was my father's,
from the land that was his father's before him,

the citizens bicker and battle
as I enter my exile, a wolf in his thicket . . .

wandering the scorched, black world . . .

Come tip a few with me,
Melanippus, and you'll see
why you crossed over Acheron
once again searching for the sun.

Come drink. Don't set your sights
too high. Even King Sisyphus—
among all men, the wisest—
thought he might outsmart Death,

only to cross Acheron twice:
the judgment of Fate.
And now he labors endlessly
in Hades.

Come drink, and celebrate
while we are young. Later,
whatever sufferings we undergo,
we will . . . the north wind blows.

I despise love. What weighty God
prefers attacks upon my heart
to shooting wild game?

And if a god consume a man in flame,
or make a trophy of his head,
what has God gained?

✛   ✛   ✛

You who were once my friend,
invited to feast on heavy wine,
succulent pork, and young lamb:

now we share only our manners.

Leaving the Peloponnese,
the sons of Leda and Zeus

call upon the great horses
of Castor and Pollux

to cross both land and sea
to rescue men who shudder below

brilliant, lightning-tipped
ship's rigging which

alternately sparks and glows,
light splashing over

the black ship . . .
black night of fear . . .

So lovely . . .
so tender . . .

they are ships . . .
and I have called after them also . . .

But whatever you give to a whore
is thrown into the pitiless gray sea,
and the man who seeks refuge
among whores will be cursed
with Sisyphean miseries.

O frail flower
of youth...

Go...

You harlot!...

✛   ✛   ✛

A poet has died.
Drink and be drunk for all time.
The window of the soul
is found in wine.

Poverty's the worst savage crime—
root of evil, pride of the damned—

who with her sister, Hopelessness,
ravages the land.

✛   ✛   ✛

Don't wait for the lamplighter,
we've still the light of dusk:
come, friend, and fill your largest cups,
as Dionysus taught us,

we'll drown our sorrows
in two parts wine, one part water,
draining this cup, then another.

. . . and if the wine leaves him witless,
his head heavy and nodding,

and if he curse his own heart for loving,
then he isn't worth noting,

his mouth overflowing
with hollow apologies . . .

ANAKREON

If Profit offered immortality for gold,
hoarding might be understandable—
a few gold coins for Thanatos,
and he'd pass on in the night.

But since a life is not for sale,
it's senseless to waste the tears.
Death, like life, is our fate.
Gold is only another emptiness.

Come, pour sweet wine for me
so we can drink, friends.
Or I might find a feather bed
and honor Aphrodite's rites.

You recount old tales of Thebes,
another recalls the warring Trojans.

I must say that I, too, was overcome,
but it was neither horse

nor army nor ship of oars
that brought me low: it was another

kind of infantry—Desire
burned me in her eyes.

Who cares about the filthy rich
excesses of the Boss of Sardis?

He's nothing to me. I won't
be bothered with tyrants.

I'm concerned with covering my head
with a garland of roses;

I'm concerned only with the moment,
tomorrow has other revisions and disclosures.

Now, under this cloudless sky,
cast your dice, pour wine for Dionysus—

soon enough a day will come
bringing consumption or diseases.

Weave garlands of roses for our hair,
and we'll get drunk on laughter;

bring a dancing girl with lovely legs,
and a sweet-lipped boy to join her;

and give him a lyre to play his song,
and Eros will follow after.

✛   ✛   ✛

Weaving a garland long ago,
somehow I found Eros
there among the roses.

I clutched him by his wings
and thrust him into wine
and drank him quickly.

And ever since, deep inside,
I feel the wings of Eros
gently tickling.

Eros, playing among the roses,
didn't see the bee.
Stung, he howled,
he screamed to Aphrodite,

"I'm dying! Mother! I'm dying!
I was bitten by
a snake with wings!"
And she kissed him and replied,

"It will pass. It was only a bee,
my darling, but think
how long the suffering
of all those who feel your sting."

✛   ✛   ✛

It is lovely to walk fields of tall grass,
the Zephyr blowing sweetly;
it is lovely to see
the tangled vines of Bacchus,

and to creep beneath their leaves
and lie in the slender arms of
a girl whose whole body
was perfumed by Kypris.

Mother Nature gave bulls horns
and gave horses hooves for speed;

she gave lions a huge mouth
and filled it with long, mean teeth;

she taught fish to swim
and gave birds the wide, high sky.

To man, she gave wisdom.
And to women? What was left?

To woman she offered a beauty
that is both a sword and a shield,

to woman a beauty
equal to fire or steel.

Count, if you can, every leaf on every tree.
And count each wave that comes ashore
    from every possible sea—
then you might number my plethora of lovers.

Compute if you can the countless loves of Athens,
the infinite passions of Korinth,
and Achaea where the women take your breath away.

Write down the names of all my loves in Lesbos,
remember their names from Ionia, from Karios
    and Rhodos,
their names from passionate dark Syria,

and from Krete where Eros runs wild in the streets.
How can I number my many loves in India,
    in Baktria?
How many did I love in Cadiz?

The dark earth drinks the sky,
and trees drink the earth.
The sea drinks the rivers,
the sun drinks the sea,
the moon drinks until
the sun goes away.

If I suggest a drink, friend,
don't quarrel with me.

✛   ✛   ✛

Spare me the man
who, pouring goblets of wine,
continues to whine all the miseries
of pestilence and war.

Bring me the one
who appreciates the plentiful
bounties of the Muses
and Aphrodite.

Bring me—at least—
a man who exalts
the ritual loveliness
of the feast.

An Eros cast in wax, molded into a candle.
When I enquired as to price,
the young vendor answered in Doric,
"He's yours, friend, at any price,
he's yours for the asking."
And said he was no real vendor,
but that for him it was a curse
to live with Eros. For a drachma,
I took the figure home and put it
in my chamber. And I told Eros,
"Consume *my* heart with fire,
or you'll go down in flames."

✛   ✛   ✛

The Muses kidnapped Eros, they bound him
in garlands and gave him away

to Beauty, and now Aphrodite,
Mother of Love, has come, bringing the bounty.

But Eros, set free, will not leave.
She's made him her slave.

Come, all you painters, all you who are the best,
you masters of Rhodian art:
My love has gone and you must paint her
exactly as I remember:

Her hair is soft—perfume your encaustic wax—
her hair is black and shining.
Under this dark hair, her sweet cheek
and brow are smooth ivory.

Above her eyes, her brows are barely parted.
Now choose
your color carefully: her eyes have the black
fire of Athena's eyes,

they are water, like Aphrodite's.
Blush of rose, skin misty smooth,
almost creamy—then leave her
lips moist with kisses.

Graceful curve of throat, like white marble,
her robe soft purple,
her body beneath it—make the robe
almost transparent—

enough! Enough. I see her. Soon,
your wax will be speaking.

Only now that my hair is gray
and my beard is white

do I realize that the grace
of youth has fled.

Even my teeth grow old
and brittle. So little time

remains. And that is why
dreams of Tartarus bring tears:

the depths of Hell burn
mightily, and the descent

itself is infinite. He
who goes will not return.

When you see my gray hair and chin,
don't run away, don't shun me.
Don't turn away, my lovely,
simply because you are young
with the blossoms of youth.

Here is my garland of roses,
all interlaced with
delicate white lilies.

✚   ✚   ✚

. . . and why
must you hurry to perfume
your heaving breast
when we all know
it is empty . . .

Artemon once traveled in shadows,
he wore a hood and earrings,
wrapped his waist in leather,
and carried a filthy shield.

He lived among beggars and whores,
often in prison or at the wheel,
the bite of the whip on his back,
his beard and hair plucked clean.

But now this son of Kykos
arrives in a woman's carriage,
gold earrings dangling,
parasol twirling, with a wink at us.

✦   ✦   ✦

Word has come to me that she
who loved so famously
lies broken-hearted, weeping
over her bitter fate,

begging the goddess to carry
her body up to a bare,
sea-beaten cliff and throw her
down into numbing waves.

LYRA

GRAECA

This altar for the Gods
was built by Sophokles
whose pain and glory were won
from the Muse of Tragedy.

– ANONYMOUS

I come tonight to sing you songs
of heroes and heroines,

to tell you tales old women tell
rich-robed girls of Tanagra—

Listen. I guarantee to please:
my song is clear and sweet.

Am I not the one who quarreled
with sweet-voiced Myrtis?

Oh, not because she's a woman!
But because she compared herself

to Pindar.

– KORINNA

Ten thousand rivers of tears,
and now, again,
Acheron, whose very name
is pain, carries
the miseries of men.

— LIKYMNIOS

It was a Phrygian, Pelops,
who first sang those songs
of the Mountain Mother,

flutes resounding
among the many wine-bowls
of drunken Greeks.

Now you hear Greeks twang,
banging on their lutes
tunes in the Lydian Mode.

— TELESTES

Hypnos, seeing how
Endymion exalted
in the light of
his true love's eyes,

taught him to sleep
with eyes open wide.

– LIKYMNIOS

It was a Phrygian king
whose immaculate breath

first tuned a flute
in the Lydian strain,

his music answering
the Dorian Muse,

weaving in his breath
inside a breeze

escaping
from a reed.

– TELESTES

On the advice of Praxilla,
we are asked to look
under every stone
for a hiding scorpion.

The proverb sounds all right.
But, turning stones,
remember:
poets also bite.

— ARISTOPHANES

Beware. There are fawns
who, facing the lion,
die of fright just thinking
the lion might be hungry.

— KYDIOS

Peeking in through
the open window,
your face was
virginal.

But you were
all woman
below.

                        – PRAXILLA

This much I know:
learn from others
their multitude
of skills.

There are no words,
invented or willed,
that were unused
before.

                        – BACCHYLIDES

Keep to the one path,
> keep to the middle,
keep to the power
> of human happiness,
don't grieve your heart to death.

Ten thousand things
> can come between
the burning heart
> and the spirit's calm,
and each asks a price for its labor.

Keep to the path.
> Study the ease.
Too much grieving
> keeps heart and soul apart.

— BACCHYLIDES

How white
her arm

as it lifts
into
a curving...

to throw...

into the
cheers of
those young men...

– BACCHYLIDES

Don't leave me
all alone. Wait

until the Morning
Star's a ghost

in the sky,
a pale white

wing carrying
the sun.

– Ion of Chios

AMATORY
POEMS

My house is simple, lying beside the sea
where I, enthroned, sun-drenched, am Queen.
All this is dear to me. But yet more dear
are those who cross these treacherous waves
in search of safety, and come to me
out of courtesy, in honor and love of Kypris:
for you, I make a gale. Sail on into grace!

— ANTIPATER OF SIDON

We who find no joy in celebrity
prefer our simple servants
to Ladies of Society
who stink of rich perfume
and put on airs. The grace
and fragrance of a servant
are her own, her bed is warm
and modest. In this,
I follow Pyrrhus, Achilles' son,
who, offered the hand of Hermione,
chose the slave Andromache.

— RUFINUS

Europa kisses sweetly,
lips barely touching lips,
but it is not the edge
of her lips that kiss:

her mouth draws out your soul,
even from your fingertips.

– RUFINUS

Something in my soul
cries, "Fly from Heliodora!
Learn from her past rages!"

But here I lie,
disgraced,
powerless to leave her.

And she, still shameless,
says, "Go!" And while she says it,
kisses.

– MELEAGER

For a little gold, Zeus bought Danae.
I, likewise, would buy you.
But I won't pay more than Zeus.

– PARMENION

Whether I see you now
with glistening raven hair

or find you blonde and fair,
I find somehow

in your sweet face
that same grace.

I daresay
the very god of love

will stroke your hair
when it is gray.

– ANONYMOUS

It's true I will die. So what do I care
whether I rot in Hell with the gout
or collapse in some damned fool race?
The same six will carry me out.

Let me limp to the end if I must.
What you get is what you see:
virtue, sin, or pleasure, I'm easy—
and I never miss a feast.

— NICARCHUS

You are a bee, my flower-lovely
Melissa! You teach me
to learn from the heart:

In the midst of our kisses,
honey drips from your lips,

and you sting me
by asking for money.

— MARCUS ARGENTARIUS

Ah, Melissa, where's your famous golden beauty,
what happened to your well-known look?

Where is your haughty, lifted brow,
your contemptuous eye and sneer?

You loved your slender neck with gold,
gold bracelets and gold anklets!

Now you're rags and dirty hair—
from queen to whore to hag,

the poetic justice of harlots.

— RUFINUS

Were that woman's postcoital charms
matched to her charms of seduction,

her lover would not lie dreaming
in another woman's arms.

— RUFINUS

Who beat you and put you out
naked in the night?

Whose heart was stone,
who gave up his eyes?

Did he discover
a secret rendezvous,

you in the arms
of your lover?

It happens. Don't cry
my child. When you've

a guest and he's away,
bolt that door!

Don't repeat
that err again.

— RUFINUS

How can any man throw out
a woman in her negligee
just because
he finds her with a lover?

As if he were an innocent!
As if he were a Pythagorean!
Don't spoil your face with tears,
my child, don't cry

outside his door. We'll find
you another lover,
a man with gentle eyes
who would never beat a child.

— RUFINUS

Her foot sparkled like silver
splashing bath water
on her golden apple breasts,
grown heavy with their milk.

Her curving hip,
smooth as water, shifted,
making waves, her hand
covering her *mons veneris,*

hiding but a part of it.

– RUFINUS

I fell in love with her kisses,
I bathed in it,

I relished, I clamored,
I longed for it.

Now I am nothing.
She is gone.

This is what love is:
love alone remembers.

– ANONYMOUS

They are too much for me,
your rosebud lips,
your mouth that makes me drunk.
Your eyes of dancing silver
snare my heart in nets.
I grow faint just dreaming
of your perfect milky breasts—
more perfect than a flower.

Saying so is telling dogs
about the nature of a bone.
I should be silent, and not
repeat the hubris of Midas.

— DIOSKORIDOS

The years have not damaged your beauty.
The temple of your youth survives.

Your ageless charm grows stronger,
a blush remains on the apple and the rose.

But think of all that passes:
the many hearts you left in ashes.

— RUFINUS

How could I have known
Kythereia was in her bath,
her lovely hands letting
her hair laugh about her throat.

May she, my queen, have mercy—
my eyes saw what was not meant for me.
Her unspeakable beauty, her graces
have shamed even the Goddess.

— RUFINUS

I like a lot of woman, full grown,
ripe or in her prime.

Young, she'll cling like clinging vine;
old, wrinkled, she'll go down.

                    – NICARCHUS

I wove this garland, Rodokleia,
with my own good hands. See,
there are violets, lilies, and roses,
narcissus and damp anemone.

Wear it wherever you go,
and leave behind your vanity,
and remember what I say:
both you and the flowers will fade.

                    – RUFINUS

Looking and lusting is not love.
He who trusts his eyes too much is blind.

But he who sees in a homely face
the beauty and the light beneath—

he knows the furnace of love's fire.
Beauty touches those who know its form.

— MARCUS ARGENTARIUS

I would be a soft pink rose
in your gentle hand, resting
on the warm snows
of your lovely breast.

— ANONYMOUS

No charm,
all looks:

she pleases
but cannot hold—

she floats like bait
without the hook.

— KAPITONOS

I can't bear to watch your hips
as you walk away.
                   Untie me!
Your thin dress leaves you
nearly naked. You tease
and tease.
          But one suggestion:
dress me, too, in gauze
so you can see
the shadow of my erection.

— MARCUS ARGENTARIUS

Left and right, I toss about my bed.
Unless you lie with me, my love,
the night brings only weariness.

– KRINAGOROS

You can explore your every desire
with Attic Europa for a dollar—
clean sheets and a warm fire
when nights grow cool.

So why, Zeus,
masquerade as a bull?

– ANTIPATER OF THESSALONICA

I'll never have a river of gold,
I'll never be a bull or a swan
with wide white wings.
Such masquerades and mythic scenes
I'll leave to tricky Zeus.

I'll rent, with these two coins,
the happiness of Korinne.

– BASSOS

Xanthippe, singing at her lyre,
with whispering eyes
sets my soul on fire.

But when? Where? How?
Everything's uncertain.
Except that my soul is burning.

— PHILODEMOS

Her perfect naked breast
upon my breast,
her lips between my lips,

I lay in perfect bliss
with lovely Antigone,
nothing caught between us.

I will not tell the rest.
Only the lamp bore witness.

— MARCUS ARGENTARIUS

You, little round-bellied,
one-eared, long-necked,
round-mouthed lover
of Bacchus and the Muses;

you, my secret treasure:
you're always full when I'm sober,
but when I'm askew, you get even.
Old friend, old jug, you abuse me.

You defy both passion and reason.

— ANONYMOUS

Where once Three Graces stood,
we now may number four:
dewy, perfumed Queen Berenika,
woman of everyone's envy—

Without you, even the Graces
are graceless.

— CALLIMACHUS

Swearing an oath to Demeter,
Nico promised to meet me tonight.

Now the first watch changes,
it is nearly midnight.

Is her word as great as her fame?
Servant! Snuff that light!

— ASKLEPIADOS

Once I lay down with Hermione
who wore a gold-stitched gown
fit for any queen.

And the song sewn round:
"Love me now and love me more
when I, with another, lay down."

— ASKLEPIADOS

Don't tell lies with your tears,
Philaenis—you love most
any lover lying close.
You love to love who is near.

— POSEIDIPPOS

In a fit, Philaenion bit me.
The bite looks slight,
but the pain is deep.

Tell all my loves
when I am gone,
Don't mourn.

Half asleep, I stepped
upon a viper.
She's bitten me, the whore!

I look
and weep
as I die.

— ASKLEPIADOS

Think how unspeakably sweet
the taste of snow at midsummer,
how sweet a kind spring breeze
after the gales of winter.

But as we all discover,
nothing's quite as sweet
as one large cloak
wrapped around two lovers.

— ASKLEPIADOS

You're in love with love,
Asklepias. With eyes as blue
as summer seas, you bemuse
and seduce all men—

stolen for love's cruises.

– MELEAGER

It is eternally winter,
these endless nights I pace
before your door, rain-
soaked, tormented
by desires fueled
by your lies, Deceiver!

It was not the kiss
of Kypris
brought me low,
but an arrow
in the heart,
hot as fire.

– ASKLEPIADOS

Love like a heavy wave,
then jealousy like stormy seas,
then winters of wine and the blues.

Tossed about like a broken boat,
I've nothing left to save.
Will I ever set eyes on you?

– MELEAGER

Nico's bedroom talents entice men
to cross the farthest seas,
she brings stripling boys
their wildest fantasies.

And then she dangles at their breast
a single translucent amethyst,
a gift from Kypris,
and a parting kiss.

– ANONYMOUS

Didyme waved an olive branch at me,
and now my heart melts like wax
embraced by flame.

Oh, I know, I know. She is dark.
And so's the coal before the spark
that makes it burn like roses.

— ASKLEPIADOS

The sounds of love are needles in my ears.
My eyes extinguish love with burning tears.

Searching for love by night and day,
I see Love folds its wings:

it will neither come
nor fly away.

— MELEAGER

Why do you stare at the floor, Chrysilla,
why must you fiddle with your skirt?
The stones that built the temple of Kypris
are made of love, not guilt.

Be silent if you must, but give me a sign, a gesture,
tell me what you've learned.

       – IRENAEUS REFERENDARIUS

They had the nerve to name you Constance,
you who fly from your lover's grip
to find yet another victim!

They love you or
they love you not,
you cruelly seduce them.

There must be fishhooks in your mouth—
once I bit, and now I hang,
bleeding from your lips.

       – MACEDONIUS

Beautiful Melite, in the throes of middle age,
retains her youthful grace.
A blush on her cheek, she seduces
with her eyes. Many years have passed,
but not her girlish laughter.
All the ravages of time cannot overcome true nature.

– AGATHIAS SCHOLASTICUS

By what right do they call Zeus a lover?
Were it so, he'd be here, among us.
Look! She's no lady-in-waiting
to Europa, to a Danae or a Leda.
Or maybe he's no use for prostitutes.
Remember: it was ignorant princesses he seduced.

– PALLADAS

That old crow-beaked hag
takes pleasure in my misery.
Neither wine nor money distracts her.

She patrols that girl like a shark.
And if the girl should steal a glance at me,
the old bitch slaps her till she cries.

Dear Persephone, take pity!
Grant us one long night
before the hag devours our hearts!

— AGATHIAS SCHOLASTICUS

Phyllis, loving Demophoon,
sent her eyes to sea.
But he, the fool,
had forgotten. And so he lied.

Now he lies alone upon the shore,
poor Demophoon,
and dreams of Phyllis who is gone,
and wonders why he cries.

— COMETAS CHARTULARIUS

My little cup, go now and taste
those honeyed lips. I, envious,
will watch and wait.

– LEONTIOS

Late last night, a girl came
and kissed me.
Her lips were sweet and wet.
And there, sipping love,
I got drunk on kisses.

– ANONYMOUS

Here is the river Eurotas,
and here is naked Leda.
There is Zeus, the swan.

And you are Cupid,
calling me on,
ready to steal my heart.

If Zeus is a swan,
what am I?
I must be a lark.

– ANTIPHILOS

PAULUS

SILENTIARIUS

How many stolen glances can we trade
and still conceal their fire?
And if we should advance to brave
a few whispered words
and are overheard, the sword
will end our pain
and dig our graves.
But if we cannot sustain
a life together, better
we should enter Hades.

✛   ✛   ✛

And now you comb and braid your hair,
and now you paint your nails.
And now you dress for someone
in the rich red purples of the sea.

But my eyes see only Rhodope,
who is somewhere far away.
And I, alone, can't even bear
to see the Morning Star.

Locked in Hippomenes' kisses,
my heart clings to Leander;

wet with Leander's lips,
Xanthus leaps to mind;

lying with Xanthus,
who should I dream but Hippomenes!

One after another,
I love my lovers,

but in the arms of each,
long for others.

Say what you will of me,
I know nothing

of love's poverty.

Come, give me kisses, Rhodope,
and honor Holy Kypris.
But please, keep our love our secret—
the honeys of secret love taste sweetest.

✝   ✝   ✝

I believe the grief of Tantalus in Hell
to be less pain than mine.

He never licked your rosebud lips
or tasted your tears of wine.

He keeps a watchful eye
but cannot die a second time.

And as I said—I, in love's ruins,
am left to envy the dead.

Galatea kisses long and wet,
Demo's mouth is pliant,
while Doris nibbles and bites.

One cannot judge by rumor,
so I taste each in turn,
determined to decide.

But I remember Demo's lips,
the honey of her tongue,
and cannot, therefore, be bribed.

Take pleasure in the others
if you will. I sink in Demo's kisses.
I make her my bride.

Sappho kisses softly,
her naked breast is soft.

But her heart is made of diamond,
love is painted on her lips.

A man who's tasted Sappho's kisses
thirsts like Tantalus.

✛   ✛   ✛

Take off your clothes, my love!
Let's get naked! I want to feel you now.

Even your gauze dressing-gown
feels thick as the walls of Babylon.

I want your lovely naked breast
against my naked breast.

Give me your lips.
Let the only veil be silence.

We are one.
Give me your tongue.

And there lay the lovers, lip-locked,
delirious, infinitely thirsting,

each wanting to go completely inside the other,
each filled to bursting with their love.

Like Achilles lying with Lycomedes,
her tunic pulled above her knees,

they grope and they fondle,
lips devouring lips, twisting like vines.

And he who is mine
trundles off to bed, thrice-blessed.

He is mine in secret only—
we burn in separate beds.

Lais smiles sweetly, and sweetly weeps.
I caressed her yesterday
and kissed away her tears,
and when I asked her why,

she said with one last shining tear,
"Please don't ever leave me!"

✦   ✦   ✦

Even clothed in wrinkles, dear Philinna,
you are more beautiful than the young.

I'd sooner taste the apples
hanging heavy from your boughs

than pinch the firm breasts of girls.
I've no taste for the young.

Your autumn outshines a mortal spring,
your winter warmer than a summer sun.

Your eyes are heavy-lidded
as though you came from bed,
your hair in tangles,
cheeks no longer red,
your body weighty.

If you've returned from
a night of love, the gift you gave
exceeds all others;
but if your lover comes only in dreams,
may all your dreams bring me.

✛   ✛   ✛

A sober man, I'll take the wine
if you are the one to bring it.

And now, before I drink it,
touch it, once, to your lips.

And *now* the cup,
foretaste of your kiss.

Why must you comment on my hair,
grown prematurely gray?
And now you say I look like I've been crying.

Is it lust or is it longing?
It's an arrow in the heart.
These long sleepless nights work me over.

My skin hangs from my flesh,
my flesh hangs from the bone,
I'm growing chins and necks.

Pity me, Lady, and love me.
Here, now, love me back my youth,
my raven hair.

✛   ✛   ✛

Bitten by a rabid dog, a man sees
the beast's face mirrored in the water.
Now love, like a mad dog, has bitten me:
I find your face in my wine cup,
I see you in the ocean depths,
you swim the slender stream.

I had Theano in bed all night,
but couldn't stop her crying.
When the Evening Star patrolled
the corridors of Heaven,
she convulsed, she cursed it
for bringing on the dawn.

Time stands for no man.
Now the night is gone.

EPIGRAMS

There's wheat at home where you didn't leave it?
You wife has a big horn of plenty.

— CALLICTEROS

No man's forever fully satisfied
fucking only his wife, my dear Charidemos.

Like you, we long for the thrill of the new.
And that accounts for our whoring.

— NICARCHUS

Apologies, dear Aphrodite. I,
who could once perform nine times,
can manage but once all night.

It looks like it's dying or dead.
I've worn the fucker out.
It looks like it's been bled.

And what have I to face
in my old age?
This last, just, disgrace.

         – PHILODEMOS

Whoa! but I stagger—too much wine!
I dance the foolish dance of Bacchus.

Together, we are three:
I carry Bacchus,
Bacchus carries me.

         – MARCUS ARGENTARIUS

I've never feared the setting of the Pleiades
or the hidden reefs beneath the waves
or even the lightning at sea

like I dread friends who drink with me
and remember what we say.

                    — ANTIPATER

Make my cup with clay—
clay that bore me to this world—
that will welcome me again.

                    — ZONAS

It's wise to make the most
of youth:
in spring a kid,
by summer a goat.

                    — ANONYMOUS

The women tease and scold me,
mocking the wreckage of my face.
It is late in my year, my snowy hair
crowns the growing dark.

I don't mind.
Perfumed and bathed,
wreathed with flowers,
I fill my cup with wine.

– PALLADAS

They whisper of you, Nicole—
they say you've dyed your hair.
I know better. It was black as coal
the very day you bought it.

– LUCILIUS

Nicole may have been a beauty long ago,
back when Moses parted the waters,
who knows? Now she's got the old ache
in the womb and wants a husband.
She ought to be looking for a tomb.

— NICARCHUS

Pity poor Philinos—young,
he married a hag;
old, he's taken a bride
of twelve or thirteen.

His Venus is always out of season.
The old lady wouldn't be bothered,
now the girl prefers
the firmer flesh of others.

— LEONIDAS

Olympikos, with your ugly face
and vanity to match Narcissus,
you ought to stay away from water—

seeing your own reflection,
you'd never forgive it.

– LUCILIUS

A weak man is like a broken jug:
although you pour in every kindness,
you pour in vain:
nothing is contained.

– LUCIAN

The vile mouth of the exorcist
drives away demons,

not by virtue of his ritual,
but by what his mouth excretes.

– LUCIAN

The poor painter captures
only form, no other.

To find the voice
you must trust color.

– LUCIAN

Little Diodoros is so skinny
that once, removing a thorn,
his own toe pierced the needle.

– NICARCHUS

A poet came to our games one day,
but when he discovered other poets,
developed laryngitis.

Now he's off to the Pythian games,
if he encounters poets there,
he'll tell them all about us.

– CEREALIOS

Eutychos was prolific as a painter
and fathered twenty sons.

And how many bore a likeness?
Not a one.

– LUCILIUS

Don't kiss the mouth of Alphaeus:
he sails the breasts of Arethusa
and drinks from her darkest sea.

– ANONYMOUS

I don't refuse that kiss
because you lick the sugar cane,
but because the sugar cane is practice.

– AMMIANUS

He, cursed with an ugly wife,
makes darkness by turning on the light.

– PALLADAS

Because you will not hear it
from the silent mirror
as you paint your counterfeit face,

I will say it for you:
in one sweet song, the poet Pindar
put it thus:

"Water is best."
He, too, disliked you.
Water is the antidote to rouge.

– MACEDONIUS

Why must you thrust your loins
against the wall, my love?
Do you think you can seduce cold stone?

– STRATO

A strange race of critics,
they perform autopsies on
the poetry of the dead.
Sad bookworms,
they chew through thorns.

No poet's too dull
for them to elucidate, these who defile
the bones of the great.
Callimachus attacked them like a dog.
Out! Into the long darkness,

perpetual beginner, little gnat—
it is a poet you distract.

                       – ANTIPHANES

A single stench two winds have parted:
has Diodoros yawned or farted?

                       – NICARCHUS

All the long evening,
talking and drinking,
those men were civilized;

but with first light in the east,
they rise to make war
like rabid beasts.

– AUTOMEDON

That poet is best
who feeds his audience
after his recitation.

Sending them home
hungry from his reading,
his talent will be questioned.

– LUCILIUS

AFTERWORD

All poetry aspires to the condition of music. Listening to the Atrium Musicae de Madrid recordings of ancient Greek music, one discovers they have made dozens of instruments replicating the originals as exactly as possible, and that many of the fragments they play are drawn from hymns and odes. There is a Pythian Ode from Pindar, Aristophanes' *Aenaoi Nephelai,* a Homeric hymn, and others. Listening, I try to imagine Catullus as he took Sappho's wedding songs (*hymenaios*) and translated them from their original Aeolic Greek into his own Latin. Sappho's *melos* resists the *melos* of Latin. *"Melos,"* Plato said, "is compounded out of three things: speech, music, and rhythm." Sappho is credited with inventing the Mixo-Lydian mode, a diatonic scale in a key corresponding to our G minor. Greek scales were all in minor key, each having a minor seventh a whole tone below the octave. It would later become known as the Gregorian Mode, Greek into Latin, and became the foundation of the "heavenly music" of the early Catholic church.

Sappho is also said by Aristoxenos to have been the

first to use the *pektis,* probably an adaptation of a stringed instrument plucked with the fingers without a plectrum by the Lydians. And indeed the Lydian *pektis* is among the instruments used by the Atrium Musicae. Listening closely, I cannot distinguish it clearly from among the other instruments, but listen again and again. I also listen for Sapphic or choriambic meters. But late, long after midnight, I realize there is little I can do to bring Sappho's *sound* into contemporary American English, except to listen and synthesize what I hear, and then make a corresponding music, embracing qualities of Plato's *melos.* Rather than concentrating strictly on her *logos,* her logic, her words, I try to find a resemblance, an echo of her music—to not present her lyrics nakedly, but to present something of her *song.*

Sappho, ancient Greek words and scales, the Latin of Catullus I wrestled with years ago—sometime after midnight, they become the koan which resolves itself, not entirely *logically,* but as a song closes with a resolve, a re-solving or re-stating of musical (emotional) pattern.

There are certain tones, certain kinds of sounds, rhythms, and repetition which seem to reach immediately into the human soul. Music, like poetry, has its roots in healing ritual and esoteric learning. In the "Judeo-Christian tradition," we find an equivalent in the form of early Talmudic scholars whose lectures were spontaneously translated into the common parlance. A culture, like a human being, achieves its greatest growth as a result of encounters with other (foreign) cultures. Sappho's Aeolian Greek is foreign even to modern Greece. But the soul is the same soul. The music, the poetry, so much of a particular time and place, transcends time and place not by articulating "original material," but by connecting to the well-springs of human experience. Octavio Paz has spoken of the classics as a "return to the source."

That innermost soul of which we are all a part resonates when touched by great music or great poetry, incantations of religious enlightenment, by the breathtaking silence and thunder of the natural world. It's in the rhythms of hard physical work fully enjoyed, in the strokes of brush on paper or canvas, it's in that song in the Bible, the Talmud, the Koran, the Rig Veda, the Lotus Sutra, the Greek Anthology, or Robert Johnson's bottleneck guitar. It's the resonance of the French poets and *philosophes* in the poetry of Wallace Stevens, the Greek, Latin, and Japanese poems buried inside Kenneth Rexroth's own autobiographical meditative longer poems, the echoes of Han Shan in Gary Snyder, the Troubadours in Pound or the revisions of Greek classics in the poetry of Hilda Doolittle. As authentically "American" as any of our poets, each articulates particular cultural-historical resonances of the unchanging human condition. While all the world around us may undergo profound transformation—for better or for worse—the fundamental human condition remains virtually unchanged over two millennia.

The stance of poets is simply an awareness of and connection—or to use Lu Chi's famous phrase: *an answering music*—to an artistic lineage. Revealing the historical traces in a poem by Eliot, by Alcaeus, or by Bashō, enriches the quality of our listening as we become increasingly aware of depth and resonance. The *listening* is the primary, but not the exclusive, text. Protinos writes:

> Invoke no operatic Muse
> nor indulge in debasing the blues—
> play both modes
> and make them true.

Several years ago, in the course of doing homework for an appreciation of Mary Barnard's translation of Sappho, I retraced the history of Sappho in English. I began carrying the Loeb Classics (Pound called them the Low Ebb Classics) and a dictionary when I traveled, making versions of Sappho, and later, others, for a small personal anthology meant for aural presentation, relying on the Loeb only for the original Greek.

I began to note certain similarities with early Japanese and Chinese poetics, especially in the poets' struggle to reveal a "personal" truth, whether in tender love song or in sorrow, in worksong or drinking song. Just as the Greeks draw on creation myths ranging from Ezra the Apocalyptist to Hermes Trismegistos, the Japanese combine Chinese Buddhist creation myths with Shinto reverence for Amaterasu Omikami. Like Sappho making her music by incorporating a borrowing from Lydian culture, the Japanese Buddhist monk enriches his *waka* (shorter poems) through his deep study of Chinese culture.

These poems, made simply for the pleasure and epiphany of the process Greeks identified as *poesis,* become *something else* once they are gathered into a single volume. Ezra Pound wrote in "The Tradition" (*Literary Essays*), "A return to origins invigorates because it is a return to nature and reason. The [one] who returns to origins does so because he [or she] wishes to behave in the eternally sensible manner. That is to say, naturally, reasonably, intuitively.... [One] wishes not pedagogy but harmony, the fitting thing."

From Sappho's 6th century B.C.E. erotic poems to their echoes in the celebratory love songs of Paulus Silentiarius in the 6th century C.E., from the earliest to the last poets of the *Greek Anthology* and the *Lyra Graeca*, I sought poems that articulate the common joys and sorrows, love and longing that are the primary metaphors of every life—poems that provide a harmony, the fitting thing.

No poem is entirely self-generating. It is a transaction between poet and muse, with a third thing—the listener—adding tension. Like jazz, translation furthers the collaborative act: the original trio becomes a quartet, requiring a certain amount of "interpretation" that results in a new harmony, but one reflecting the nature of the original.

The fundamental experiences of humanity remain simultaneously universal and particular. The tears of Lymnos on the banks of the Acheron are the same tears Hitomaro shed a thousand years later on the shores of the Omi Sea. East and west, north and south, we are not as different as we may like to believe. Somewhere between the marketplace of the *polis* and the boudoir of the megalopolis, between the *symposion* (drinking party) of Anakreon and late 20th-century suburbia, we encounter the same moon, alone, passing through. And we are suddenly moved, surprised by our own capacity for love and anger, companionship and loneliness.